W9-BXW-405

Ladybugs

ABDO
Publishing Company

Julie Murray

Big Buddy BOOKS
Insects

VISIT US AT
www.abdopublishing.com

Published by ABDO Publishing Company, 8000 West 78th Street, Edina, Minnesota 55439.

Printed in the United States of America, North Mankato, Minnesota.
042010
092010

 PRINTED ON RECYCLED PAPER

Coordinating Series Editor: Rochelle Baltzer
Editor: Sarah Tieck
Contributing Editors: Heidi M.D. Elston, Megan M. Gunderson, BreAnn Rumsch, Marcia Zappa
Graphic Design: Maria Hosley
Cover Photograph: *iStockphoto*: ©iStockphoto.com/ABV.
Interior Photographs/Illustrations: *AnimalsAnimals-EarthScenes*: ©BEATTY, BILL (pp. 13, 27), © DEGGINGER, E. R. (pp. 11, 15, 21, 30), ©LAYER, WERNER (p. 10), ©MURRAY, PATTI (p. 17), ©SPECKER, DONALD (pp. 10, 13); *iStockphoto*: ©iStockphoto.com/Alex_Ishchenko (p. 27), ©iStockphoto.com/Antagain (pp. 5, 7); ©iStockphoto.com/dabjola (p. 11), ©iStockphoto.com/Gala_Kan (p. 27), ©iStockphoto.com/GlobalP (p. 5), ©iStockphoto.com/jamesrudge (p. 15), ©iStockphoto.com/laughingmango (p. 29), ©iStockphoto.com/macroworld (p. 11), ©iStockphoto.com/MAYBAYBUTTER (p. 30), ©iStockphoto.com/robgr85 (p. 19), ©iStockphoto.com/w-ings (p. 25), ©iStockphoto.com/wayra (p. 23), ©iStockphoto.com/whitemay (p. 11); *John Foxx Images* (pp. 9, 15); *Stockbyte* (p. 15).

Library of Congress Cataloging-in-Publication Data

Murray, Julie, 1969-
 Ladybugs / Julie Murray.
    p. cm. -- (Insects)
 ISBN 978-1-61613-487-7
 1. Ladybugs--Juvenile literature. I. Title. II. Series: Murray, Julie, 1969- Insects.
 QL596.C65M873 2011
 595.76'9--dc22
                              2010002527

Contents

Insect World

Millions of insects live throughout the world. They are found on the ground, in the air, and in the water. Some have existed since before there were dinosaurs!

Ladybugs are one type of insect. They live in wooded areas and grassy fields around the world. If you look closely, you might find ladybugs in your backyard!

Bug Bite!

Ladybugs are a type of beetle. They are sometimes called lady beetles or ladybird beetles.

Ladybugs have many different colors and patterns.

A Ladybug's Body

Most ladybugs are less than one-half inch (1 cm) long. Like all insects, they have three main body parts. These are the head, the **thorax**, and the **abdomen**.

A ladybug's head has two eyes, two antennae, and a mouth. Its mouth has small, sharp **jaws** for chewing.

Six legs connect to the ladybug's thorax. The thorax also has two pairs of wings. Important **organs** are inside the abdomen.

Bug Bite! One part of the thorax is called the pronotum. The pronotum protects and hides a ladybug's head.

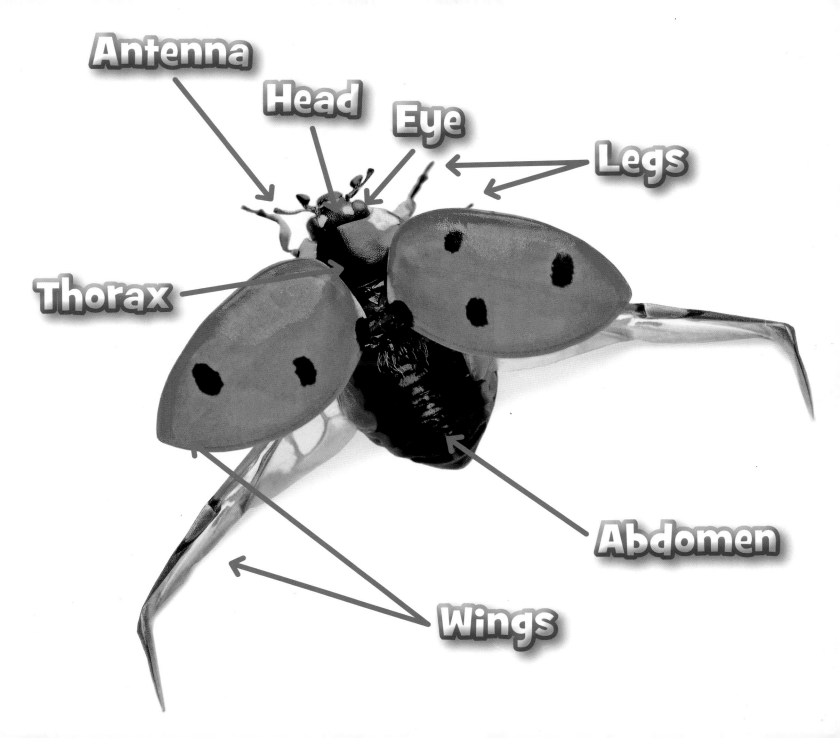

Antenna

Head

Eye

Legs

Thorax

Abdomen

Wings

Fly Away with Me

Adult ladybugs move by flying and crawling. They have two pairs of wings. To fly, ladybugs flap their soft inner wings.

A ladybug's hard outer wings are called elytra (EH-luh-truh). These wings are also very important. They **protect** the ladybug's body.

Ladybugs flap their wings about 85 times per second when flying!

Beautiful Lady

Ladybugs are famous for their looks. Most people think they are red or orange with black spots. But, ladybugs may be red, orange, yellow, white, pink, or black! And, not all of them have spots.

In the insect world, bright colors often mean something is poisonous. So, many predators stay away from ladybugs.

Two common North American ladybugs are the convergent ladybug (*left*) and the seven-spotted ladybug (*right*).

There are more than 4,500 species of ladybugs in the world.

Ladybugs have many different colors and markings on their wings.

One of a Kind

Each ladybug has different markings. Even within the same **species**, ladybugs have slightly different appearances. Their color and markings may fade over time.

Bug Bite!

Some people believe ladybugs bring good luck. These insects appear in many stories.

The eye-spotted ladybug *(left)* and the parenthesis ladybug *(below)* are named for their markings.

Life Begins

The ladybug life cycle has four stages. These are egg, larva, pupa, and adult.

Like other insects, all ladybugs begin life as eggs. After **mating**, the female ladybug often lays her eggs on the underside of a leaf. She chooses a plant near many tiny bugs called aphids. That way, the baby ladybug will have food to eat.

Bug Bite!

Some ladybugs lay more than 1,000 eggs in a lifetime.

Life Cycle of a Ladybug

Egg

Larva

Pupa

Adult

Growing Up

A larva grows inside each egg. In a few days, the eggs **hatch** and the larvae crawl out.

When they are born, ladybug larvae don't look like adults. They have long bodies with long legs and no wings. Their heads have strong **jaws** for biting and chewing food.

Right after they hatch, some larvae eat their eggshells.
Then, they look for tiny bugs called aphids to eat.

Ladybug larvae are very hungry. For a couple of weeks, they eat and eat. They grow and change quickly. As they grow, they become too big for their skin. So, they shed their skin. This is called molting. Larvae molt many times.

Bug Bite!

The ladybug is the state insect of Delaware, Massachusetts, New Hampshire, Ohio, and Tennessee.

A larvae's skin feels very tight right before it sheds. Shedding old skin uncovers new skin underneath it.

Becoming a Ladybug

After a couple of weeks, a ladybug larva stops eating. It attaches itself to a leaf, a stick, or a rock. Then, a shell covers its soft body. It is now in the pupa stage.

Inside a pupa, an adult ladybug forms. Then, the shell splits open. An adult ladybug comes out. Over time, its markings begin to show.

Pupa cannot escape predators. But sometimes, they can scare them away by jerking suddenly.

Adult ladybugs can live for more than one year. This is longer than many insects live. Ladybugs **hibernate** during the cold winter months. When it is warm, they eat, **mate**, and lay eggs.

Bug Bite!

Ladybugs choose hidden places to hibernate. They like to hide beneath rocks, under decks, and inside rotting logs.

Some ladybugs gather in large groups called swarms to hibernate. It helps them stay warm.

Big Eater

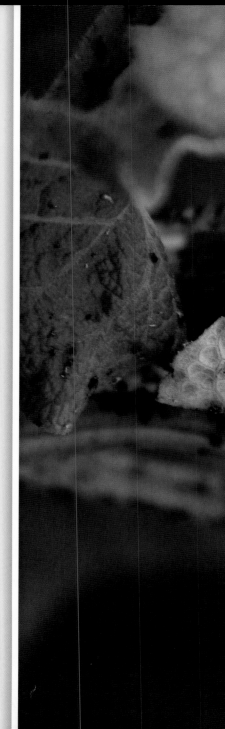

Adult ladybugs are strong predators. They hunt and catch tiny bugs. These include aphids, scales, and mites.

A ladybug needs a lot of food to survive. It might eat 5,000 insects in its life! If there is not enough food, it flies somewhere else.

Aphids are also called plant lice. They harm plants by sucking out their juices. If not controlled, aphids can destroy entire fields of plants.

Danger Zone

During their lives, ladybugs face predators. These include other insects, birds, and frogs.

Ladybugs have ways to **protect** themselves. Their bright colors are a warning. If they are attacked, a smelly liquid comes out of their legs. It tastes bad to many predators. Ladybugs may also play dead to trick enemies.

Praying mantises *(left)* and spiders *(right)* eat ladybug larvae and adult ladybugs.

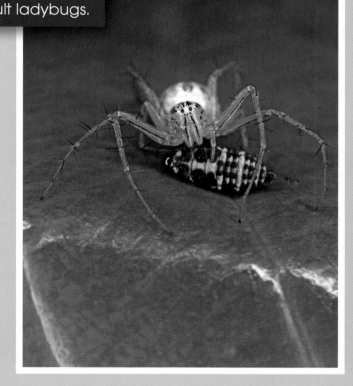

Aphids produce a liquid that ants like to eat. So, ants may attack ladybugs to protect aphids.

Special Insects

Ladybugs help keep the natural world in balance. They serve as food for some animals. And, they eat insects that harm gardens and farms. In this way, they **protect** crops. Ladybugs are important insects.

Bug Bite!

To help control pests, farmers can buy ladybugs by the gallon. One gallon (4 L) includes about 70,000 ladybugs!

The bugs that ladybugs eat are considered pests. So, the ladybug is a helpful predator.

Bug-O-Rama

What is something surprising about ladybugs?

The Volkswagen Beetle car got its name from ladybugs. It looks like a ladybug! Some people even call these cute, round cars "bugs."

Do any ladybugs eat plants?

Some ladybugs eat plants instead of insects. These include the squash beetle and the Mexican bean beetle. Farmers try to keep them away from their crops.

How far do ladybugs travel?

Most don't go too far. But in 1999, four ladybugs went into space! They traveled on a shuttle with astronauts. There, they were part of science experiments.

Important Words

abdomen (AB-duh-muhn) the back part of an insect's body.

hatch to be born from an egg.

hibernate to sleep or rest during the winter months.

jaws a mouthpart that allows for holding, crushing, and chewing.

mate to join as a couple in order to reproduce, or have babies.

organ a body part that does a special job. The heart and the lungs are organs.

protect (pruh-TEHKT) to guard against harm or danger.

shed to cast aside or lose as part of a natural process of life.

species (SPEE-sheez) living things that are very much alike.

thorax the middle part of an insect's body.

Web Sites

To learn more about ladybugs, visit ABDO Publishing Company online. Web sites about ladybugs are featured on our Book Links page. These links are routinely monitored and updated to provide the most current information available.

www.abdopublishing.com

Index